turn, climb, realign

Yavanika Press

turn, climb, realign

Cover photo: Karthik Ranganathan

First published in 2019 by Yavanika Press
Bangalore, India

Copyright © 2019 Samar Ghose

All rights reserved. This book or any portion thereof may not be reproduced or used in any manner whatsoever without the express written permission of the publisher, except for the use of brief quotations in a book review.

ISBN: 9781689126007

For
lipi & tiggy
my raison d'être

Acknowledgements

I would like to extend my thanks to the editors of the following publications in which present or earlier versions of these haibun sequences previously appeared: *Haibun Today*, *Human/Kind Journal*, *The Other Bunny*, and *weird laburnum*.

turn, climb, realign

serry

partly cloudy, just

cold

weight
of the
mood

ring

*

turning over you get a sudden memory in your head

tea
leaves

the
book lamp
dims

*

another idea grips you

inchworm
now

or

*

thinking about tomorrow, like you've abandoned its trajectory already

the dancer's fingers rake the moon

tabula rasa

some who are near my heart

the song
in turn
is born

*

with one purpose alone

a stone
changes
within

*

minute by minute they live

a heart murmur
run
wild

dark and light

a cosmetic facade, the face saved, bruise concealed :: today she wears a bright white singlet

ten thousand volumes
dust
streaks the empty couch

*

the war rages on, a spreading dark water-stain :: her gentle brand of distracted kindness

the palm opens a dream a dream to closing time

*

seconds. minutes. light :: the last remaining cupcake in crumbs sequencing a daydream

the geese
turn
climb
realign
above the checkerboard

so to speak

coming in with his wandering eyes :: the pain routinely questioned

when is it
that it is
no time

*

his words riding a familiar tilt :: bootlaces trailing

one sparrow two the cerulean bit by bit

*

a certain ennui, a certain languor :: a door across the hall ticks open

departing geese letting the night in

*

a spider hangs from the rafters :: bits of poems

as if Pandora reciting the sutras, so to speak

fraught

missing

a dog
strips the air
of fright

*

there is no breeze

trapped
the bruise
of a sky

*

she knows, she knows

no sound
is silent now

Androméda

a small parenthesis—she took it and raised her glass to express the emotion of the song

perfect figure eights on an inward-looking arrhythmia

*

by then, the afternoon outside was gathering into bluey darkness

night sounds
a fishhook breaks the surface
to applause

*

growing less insistent until there were only fireflies

touch and go nights falling down the rabbit hole

*

in search of body heat, quite naturally my arm went around her

the nebula
of another galaxy
passes through

distal pulse

phone call from the psych—she's taken it badly. I know, I say.

the climb
for the moon
not this
not this

*

about to wrap myself in her scarf, I stop. What if I lose my sense of her?

worse
things

I tell
myself

happen
at sea

*

the truculence of children :: on and off the rain

jumpers
do they see the sky
above

penumbra

listening to the growing quiet of the night

just
this one time
faucet

*

in the small hours, the first jumbos

in me
the ancient
me

*

the roar of their engines like a slowly breaking wave as they wheel and bank in over the city

I
Kant
never
the
less

enough

the trouble with marbles is the rich kid doesn't give them back when your kid brother chucks them over

three bags full
yuk, what do they
call this stuff

*

downstream, the call of a bird, maybe, but stop at nothing while it's still dark

grandma
you had to be
it

*

hard up against it with nowhere else to go, there's just the crunch of gravel

they
wouldn't
want
to be
built

walls would

if
they
could
speak

, which space is, unless…

a framed pane of clear glass :: infinity keeping, keeping

in and out of the bird feeder

*

changing light :: collecting parts of a visual wall less the night

look inside

the
dream

writing the years

*

night out, you open the can :: 5 years through the pupil of an empty space

the eye
now a familiar
raga
unfamiliar

*

escape the tomorrow :: ribbon clouds expanding a splinter you can slip into

old glass
fears distort
into dust

an absolutely ordinary rainbow

the word goes round :: scribblers forget the chalk in their hands

the cry
stops the rain
hurrying

*

talk in the back streets minutes ago :: around a child like the wind in a hollow

midday light
uniforms crowd
a halo

*

a thing some say wills man :: there the slick silence burns

like the earth
as the earth
the sea stops

memory

the squares of his mind scattered cities :: another code of a dead man living

in the morrow
the cell
of this day

*

one thinks of something slightly unusual :: silly, like us, her madness survives

making south
in the dark
the dogs wait

*

hate the sea of the night :: your voice still a vineyard of praise

a verse
deserts
the fountain

Notes

'fraught': A sequence culled out from p. 41 of *Rhubarb* by Craig Silvey.

'tabula rasa': A sequence culled out from *Easter, 1916* by W. B. Yeats.

'an absolutely ordinary rainbow': A sequence culled out from *An Absolutely Ordinary Rainbow* by Les Murray.

', which space is, unless…': A crowdsourced sequence composed from responses/definitions received for the concrete noun, "window."

'memory': A sequence culled out from *In Memory of W. B. Yeats* by W. H. Auden.

Samar Ghose was born and grew up in India. He now lives in Perth, Western Australia with his wife and two adult daughters. Enamoured of the haiku genre and its related forms, he enjoys the appreciation of this art form while reading and occasionally writing. He has been published in international online and print journals such as *Sonic Boom*, *weird laburnum*, *Human/Kind Journal*, *The Heron's Nest*, *Under the Basho*, *Haibun Today*, *Bones*, *The Other Bunny*, and numerous others. Samar feels that haiku can live in both poetry and prose and explores the conceptual possibilities of haikai aesthetics through the writing of mini-haibun sequences.

Made in the USA
Middletown, DE
13 September 2019